Twelve Months To Live

A Guide For Transformation

By

Eric A. Sleith III
LPCC, NCC, ACS

ISBN # 978-1456477691

Eric A. Sleith III, LPCC, NCC, ACS, is a Licensed Professional Clinical Counselor, National Certified Counselor and an Approved Clinical Supervisor. Eric has worked in the fields of counseling & human services for nearly two decades. In addition, he was a college professor for over 10 years, where he served as a counselor educator.

Additional Publications

Sleith, Eric (2010). *That's How the Fortune Cookie Crumbles.*

Sleith, Eric (2010). *You & Me = We.*

Sleith, Eric (201?). *Dark Horse: Stories about Defying Gravity.*

Sleith, Eric (201?). *Beyond Frugal: Lessons on Dollars & Uncommon Cents.*

Sleith, Eric (2011). *Duality of Personality.*

Sleith, Eric (2007). 3rd Edition. *Embracing & Transcending Death, Loss, & Grief.*

Sleith, Eric, et al., (2008). 2nd Edition. *Common Terms & Concepts in Counseling & Psychology.*

I would like to dedicate this book to my wife Amy and my daughter Morgan.

Dear Amy,

For someone that has been through so much, I am amazed that you still have such a kind heart. You inspire me to become a better person, and I am blessed to have you in my life!

Dear Morgan,

Someday, after I am gone, you will read this book and I want you to remember that it's okay to be sad. But don't get lost in your grief. If you will allow death to be your teacher, you'll learn many important lessons about life. My hope is that you will embrace life and not take a single moment for granted. I will see you again one day, but until then, live every moment like it's your last. And always remember that I love you with all my heart!

I would like to express my sincere gratitude to the following people.

Amy Sleith, Morgan Sleith, Brian Cunningham, Dan Zehnder, Dave McNeely, Daya Sandhu, Todd Nichols, Doug Des Ruisseaux, Geoff Hushaw.

Contents

Introduction

Chapters:

1. What's Most Important: *Your Central Life Goal*
2. Relationship (with self & others)
3. Toxic Thoughts & Emotions
4. Physical Health
5. Spirituality
6. Occupation & Avocation
7. Get Your Financial House in Order
8. Plan Your Own Funeral
9. Top Ten List

Afterword
Checklist

This _workbook_ should not be solely read for content. It is intended to be experienced and worked through. With this in mind, please allow enough time to reflect and complete the numerous experiential exercises.

Introduction

This workbook was written for anyone that is seeking profound structural change in their life. Someone that has received a terminal diagnosis can obviously utilize this material, but it is by no means restricted to this category. The length of time we have in this world is limited, so we must strive to develop more love and create meaning with what we have been given. I would like to share a profound statement that will help the reader to view this workbook within an existential context.

"Death and life are interdependent, and though physical death destroys us, the idea of death saves us."

~ Irvin D. Yalom

Keep this existential concept in mind as you proceed through the exercises in this workbook. This material was not created to glorify death or suggest a preoccupation with the morbid, but to bring *life* into sharper focus, through the realization of the finite.

Imagine for a moment that you are in your car. It's a rainy day and the road is slippery. Suddenly your car spins out of control and when it finally stops, you find yourself facing a large oncoming truck. It feels like time stands still, and then you realize – *it's your time!*

Then, something absolutely miraculous occurs. At the last moment, the truck swerves to the other lane and your life is spared. Afterwards, you feel like you're walking in a dream-like state, where everything looks surreal. It's as if you are moving between two separate realities, one of the living, and one of the dead. And then it hits you; you have been given another chance at life. How will you live differently, and what changes will you make?

It doesn't have to take a near death experience to inspire change. Right at this very moment you can choose to follow a different path. But you must commit to the pursuit of a new dream, and walk away from a passageway that fits like a worn-out, yet familiar pair of jeans. This workbook can help you to recognize what's most dear to your heart and then provide structured exercises to help facilitate transformation.

All changes, even the most longed for, have their melancholy; for what we leave behind us is a part of ourselves; we must die to one life before we can enter another.

~Anatole France

Only birth can conquer death — the birth, not of the old thing again, but of something new. When our day is come for the victory of death, death closes in; there is nothing we can do, except be crucified — and resurrected; dismembered totally, and then reborn.

~Arnold J. Toynbee
As quoted by Joseph Campbell

Chapter 1

Your work is to discover your world and then with all your heart give yourself to it.

~Buddha

1. What is the central motivating force in your life?

2. What do you most desire your life to stand for?

3. What would you like your legacy to be?

Please answer these questions on the following page.

1. _____

   _____

   _____

   _____

2. _____

   _____

   _____

   _____

3. _____

   _____

   _____

   _____

Are your *actions* moving you *closer to or further away* from your stated purpose and objectives? If your behavior is consistent with your aspiration, then please continue. If not, what do you need to change?

_____

_____

_____

_____

_____

_____

_____

_____

_____

_____

_____

A *mission statement* is a brief written declaration that serves the purpose of guiding the actions of a company or organization. It clearly defines the overarching principles, provides a sense of direction, and organizes the decision making process. Without a mission statement, a company would lack a stable sense of identity and direction. For better or worse, they would move in whatever direction the wind blows. Although most people acknowledge the importance of a mission statement in the business arena, they are unaware of its significance in their personal lives.

When a man does not know what harbor he is making for, no wind is the right wind.

~Seneca

As an example, I will share my own personal mission statement. This will provide you with a template to follow when creating your own on the following page.

Eric's Mission Statement

I will build a life that is filled with love, joy, peace, meaning, and kindness. I will live in the *"present moment"* - with an identity that is derived from *who I am*, and not from what I do or possess. I will *"create"* things such as: books, art, photos, music, etc. And I will share my creations with others, so they may be inspired, challenged, and encouraged.

Create Your Own Mission Statement

_____

_____

_____

_____

_____

_____

_____

_____

_____

_____

_____

_____

What if you only had twelve-months to live?

How would you live the last year of your life? Is there anything you would do different? We never know how much time we have left in this world!

_____

_____

_____

_____

_____

_____

_____

_____

_____

Few people succeed at anything of value without setting goals. There is something powerful about setting a goal and then putting it in *writing*. There's a sense of accountability and realism when we get an idea out of our head and write it down on paper.

Goals are divided into three categories. First, there are *long-term goals*. They serve the purpose of *directing* an overall strategy. Long terms goals are related to the *mission statement* that was described in the previous exercise, but they differ in one important aspect. A mission statement describes who you want to be and what you want to do, while long-term goals outline the steps needed to get there. In other words, it delineates in specific detail how you plan to make your dream a living reality. Long-term goals look to the future and are concerned with the grand scheme of things. Next, medium-term goals pertain to implementing the overall strategy at the midpoint of a project. Lastly, short-term goals focus upon day-to-day execution of the overarching mission, just as the name implies.

I view goal setting as analogous to writing a paper or dissertation. When writing, you begin with an opening statement that describes what the paper is about. Subsequent paragraphs further elaborate and reinforce the overall topic at different time intervals, which finally culminates at the conclusion of the paper.

A goal should never be viewed as something that is written in stone. Flexibility and adaptation to the current situation is vital. In addition, the phrase *long-term* is defined differently for each person and circumstance. For example, a long-term goal may be six to twelve months, or twenty to thirty years.

Now it's time for you to describe in specific detail how you plan to make your mission statement a reality and not just a dream. On the following page, write down your long, medium, and short-term goals.

Long-term goals

_____

_____

_____

_____

Medium-term goals

_____

_____

_____

_____

Short-term goals

_____

_____

_____

_____

A person will sometimes devote his life to the development of one part of his body – the wishbone.

~Robert Frost

In order to achieve your goals you must move beyond *wishful thinking*. What steps must you take in order to implement your goals?

Take time to reflect.

Now

Take action!

Chapter 2

Be who you are and say what you feel, because those who mind don't matter and those who matter don't mind.

~Dr. Seuss

Before you can have meaningful relationships with others, you must first have a genuine relationship with yourself. However, this is far more difficult than you may imagine. We are born into the world with a natural sense of wonder! For the most part, we are comfortable in our own skin and our *true self* has not yet been suppressed. As we grow older, we are molded into something that may significantly deviate from our true self. This occurs because we adhere to societal standards and the expectations of significant others. A few examples, which illustrate this point, are sexual identity and orientation, career choice, religious affiliation, etc.

I am not suggesting that the socialization process is all bad or unnecessary. Without learning about rules of behavior it would be difficult to function in society at all. But at some point, it seems that most of our dreams are stripped away and we are told to *face reality*. So we create a persona in order to fit in and to receive validation from those around us. So as long as we do not lose touch with our true self, there is nothing wrong with creating masks in order to fulfill different roles (e.g. teacher, father, mother, doctor, etc.) But for many, these masks become our identity and we forget who we really are.

People often ask the infamous question: "What do you do?" But a far more important inquiry that is rarely explored, solicits an answer to a much deeper question.

"<u>Who are you?</u>"

I once heard a story about a man that was very wealthy and successful. However, this man did not just pursue his own self-interests, but took great pride in helping others too. One day after leaving the office, he decided to stop at a restaurant for a quick meal. When the employees saw him drive up in his expensive sports car, they raced to take his order. They treated him special because they wanted a big tip, but they also sought to be seen with such a triumphant person. They unconsciously believed that they'd become more desirable if they were associated with him, even for just a moment.

The following week this man was volunteering at a local homeless shelter. He was dressed casually and drove the shelter's work truck so he could pick up restoration materials from the hardware store. He knew that it would be a long day of hard work so he decided to stop and get some food. He pulled into the very same restaurant parking lot that he had patronized the week before. But this time he had a very different experience.

What had changed about this man? Although he wore sweat pants and drove an old truck, was he not the same person from the previous week?

We've all heard stories about the physically attractive model that gets into an accident and is no longer perceived as beautiful. Or the person with superior cognitive abilities that loses the admiration of others after experiencing a severe brain injury. What happens when the roles and attributes that we so deeply identify with (smart, sexy, wealthy, hard-working, etc.) are torn away? I make this point to get you to consider the fundamental question concerning your identity, beyond any achieved or ascribed roles (or lack thereof).

Who are you?

If you had one year left, would you continue to live your life based on the expectations of others?

Are you living a life filled with personal integrity and authenticity?

Are you being true to your _real self_?

On this page, draw a picture of your persona, or false self that you project to others. Then on the following page, draw a picture of your *true self*. You may substitute descriptive words instead of drawing.

False Self

True Self

Is there any incongruence between your persona and your real self? Would you like to alter this in some way?

_____

_____

_____

_____

_____

_____

_____

_____

_____

_____

_____

_____

_____

_____

_____

_____

_____

_____

_____

_____

_____

_____

Take time to reflect.

Now that we have acknowledged the importance of having an authentic relationship with self, I'd like to switch gears and focus on the topic of relationships with others. Oftentimes we hold on to anger and resentment long after a harmful incident has occurred. We do this because we want justice, or if we're honest, vengeance. Emotional reactions such as anger and rage are natural, and nothing to be ashamed of. But we must keep in mind that these feelings can become toxic and poison our mind, body and spirit.

There is a wise saying that states, *"Forgiveness brings freedom and healing to the survivor."* Many times people misinterpret this idea and falsely believe that forgiveness is synonymous with letting the other person off the hook. Nothing could be further from the truth. When possible, the perpetrator must be held accountable. But forgiveness in the *heart* is always essential for healing. For instance, I have provided consultation for **MADD** (Mothers Against Drunk Drivers). I observed numerous judges that ruled in favor of shock probation and community service after a drunk driver had killed an innocent person(s). Not only did the families of the deceased have to deal with the grief of losing their loved one(s), but they were further victimized by the judicial system. I must admit that I found it difficult to discuss forgiveness, while there was such an utter lack of **accountability!** *(Note ~ Forgiveness is not something that should be encouraged in the beginning stages of the recovery process. Feelings of rage and betrayal must be allowed to surface and then dealt with in a productive manner).* **Nevertheless, in the long run, I believe that forgiveness is ultimately the only way to transcend such trauma.**

Let me share a less emotionally charged example that will further illustrate my point. I have a friend that plays the electric guitar. Many years ago, a roommate stole his vintage 6-string. Not only was this instrument worth a great deal of money, but it also had enormous sentimental value. Some years later, the person that stole the guitar approached my friend and asked for his forgiveness. He said that he was a drug abuser and had stolen the guitar to support his addiction. The twelve-step recovery model that he was involved in instructed him to make things right with those who he had harmed. My friend explained the situation and asked for my opinion on what he should do. I described the powerful gift of forgiveness and how it could release both the victim and perpetrator from the grips of hatred and despair. Then I went on to say something that my friend did not expect. I told him that he should forgive, regardless of the outcome, but still hold the thief responsible for his crime. In other words, the perpetrator must agree to give him enough money to purchase an equivalent guitar that will replace the one stolen. My friend asked, "What if he won't repay me, then what should I do?" I simply said, you should still forgive him, but if he won't set up a payment plan, then his crime must be reported to law enforcement.

Sometimes people also falsely believe that forgiveness means reconnecting with someone that has harmed you. Although forgiveness can bring about reconciliation, this is not always the case. In fact, setting healthy boundaries and separating from a chaotic and toxic environment can be a vital part of the internal process of healing and forgiveness. Surrounding yourself with positive and healthy people, while at the same time divorcing yourself from chaos, will allow you to create a space in which forgiveness is possible.

Are there any relationships that you would like to repair before leaving this world? Do you need to forgive someone? Do you need to ask someone to forgive you? Have you outgrown certain people or situations? If so, do you need to move on or set healthy boundaries concerning if/when/how you will be involved? Below, please provide answers to these important questions.

_____

_____

_____

_____

_____

_____

Every time I attend a funeral service I'm struck by the juxtaposition of a cold lifeless body and the vibrant colors and aromatic scents from a menagerie of flowers. I also find it interesting how people eulogize the dead to the point of unrealistic idealization, even though they offered little praise and encouragement while the person was alive. Did the deceased receive a bountiful supply of kind words and beautiful flowers while living, or did friends and family wait to express kindness and appreciation until the time of death?

What is holding you back from showing sensitivity and compassion to those you care about?

_____

_____

_____

I encourage you (and me) to try a little experiment. Pick or purchase some flowers for someone you care about "today" instead of waiting until their funeral. (Trust me, one less bouquet will not be missed at the cemetery, and the person will get to enjoy them while living.) Or write a heartfelt letter that lets the person know how much you admire and appreciate them, etc.

<u>Examples:</u>

Monday: Mom & Dad / Make them dinner.

Tuesday: Best Friend / Hand written letter.

Sunday:_____

_____

Monday:_____

_____

Tuesday:_____

_____

Wednesday:_____

_____

Thursday:_____

_____

Friday:_____

_____

Saturday:_____

_____

Chapter 3

Although I'm not where I want to be, I celebrate I'm not where I used to be.

~Eric A. Sleith III

This chapter is devoted to addressing the topics of self-defeating thoughts and venomous emotions, which can increase our stress level and adversely affect our well-being. I'd like to begin by focusing upon a fascinating area of interdisciplinary medical research called psychoneuroimmunology. After reading this large and intimidating word you may be tempted to skip this chapter, but I encourage you to continue reading.

I realize that the term psychoneuroimmunology can be quite a tongue twister, so let's break this word down into more manageable pieces. *Psycho is derived from the word psychology.* The root of the word psychology (psukho) means "spirit" or "soul" in Greek. Until the end of the 19th century psychology was regarded as a branch of philosophy, which focused upon religious and metaphysical phenomena. It later evolved into a pure science that studied mental processes and behavior. *Neuro is derived from the word neurology.* This branch of medicine deals with the nervous system and disorders affecting it. *Immunology* is the branch of biomedicine that deals with the structure and function of the immune system.

Now let's bring all the parts of this word back together and create a useful definition. Psychoneuroimmunology is the field that deals with the interaction between the psychological state and the nervous and immune systems of the human body.

I have underscored this area of research because it illustrates the powerful influence that thoughts and emotions have on the physical body. There is a plethora of empirically supported research that demonstrates how stress reduction, optimism, positive thinking, etc. can influence healing and prevent disease. Unfortunately, the inverse is also just as powerful. (See references below)

1. Herbert TB, Cohen S. Stress and immunity in humans: a meta-analytic review. Psychosomatic Medicine. 1993;55:364–379.

2. Zorrilla, E. P., Luborsky, L., McKay, J. R., Rosenthal, R., Houldin, A., Tax, A., McCorkle, R., Seligman, D. A., & Schmidt, K. (2001). The relationship of depression and stressors to immunological assays: a meta-analytic review. Brain Behavior and Immunity, 15(3), 199-226.

Rene Descartes is a famous philosopher who is credited with the development of the idea of a mind/body dualism or Cartesian dualism. Descartes believed that the mind and body are separate or dichotomous parts. In other words, if someone has a problem with a body part or bodily function, it is mitigated by the use of chemical and/or mechanical interventions, while emotional and psychological factors are disregarded. This theory has had a profound affect on the practice of medicine. Unfortunately, many physicians and other professionals within the medical community still adhere to this antiquated view. Others practicing the healing arts have gone to the other extreme and will sometimes tell patients that the reason they're sick is because they are doing it to themselves, or it's all in their "head." From my perspective, both positions are incorrect and extremely damaging to the *person* seeking assistance. There is a reciprocal influence between the mind and body. For example, when your stomach hurts, it affects how you feel emotionally and influences your thoughts and perceptions. Conversely, if your become clinically depressed, it affects the body (e.g. muscle & joint pain, restlessness, etc.)

At this point you might be asking yourself, "What does this have to do with me and my situation?" I hope by now I have made a good case for the interconnectedness of the mind, body and some would say "spirit." Please take some time to consider this information and then answer the questions on the following pages.

Are there any self-destructive thoughts or noxious emotions that *consistently* affect you? If you knew you were going to die soon, would there be any issues you'd like to address before transitioning into the after life or your next life? If so, what steps must you take to begin the healing process?

_____

_____

_____

_____

_____

_____

_____

_____

_____

_____

_____

_____

_____

_____

_____

_____

_____

_____

_____

_____

_____

* It feels good to talk with a supportive friend. But sometimes it's helpful to speak with an objective & caring professional. This chapter is not intended to take the place of a comprehensive assessment by a licensed mental health counselor.

Chapter 4

Our body is merely a shell, which houses the soul. But just like the tortoise, we need an outer layer to protect our core.

~Eric A. Sleith

As I write this chapter, I am mindful that some readers may be in very poor health with literally twelve months to live. Others may not have a terminal diagnosis, but avoid the necessary steps to ensure good health. Regardless of your situation, I believe this chapter has something of value to offer. It may need to be adjusted to fit your individual circumstance, but the underlying theory can still be generalized.

Good physical health is vital for an overall sense of well-being. If you've ever been ill or experienced intense pain, then you know first-hand how it can affect every aspect of your life (i.e. emotional, relational, occupational, etc.) Our culture has an interesting relationship with physical health and fitness. Many are completely unconcerned with such matters and neglect their body's most basic needs, while others are consumed with mimicking the cultural ideals (e.g. thinness) to the point of starvation and self-harm. Both extremes are detrimental and do not reflect good physical health. For the purposes of this book, it is necessary to explicitly define what I mean by physical health. Rather than promote a definition based on the current flavor of the week, I will quote the World Health Organization. In 1986, the (WHO) World Health Organization in the Ottawa Charter for Health Promotion defined health as, "A resource for everyday life, not the objective of living. Health is a positive concept emphasizing social and personal resources, as well as physical capacities."

I like this definition because it focuses upon physical health as a means to an end, and not an end, in and of itself. In addition, it reinforces the intrapersonal and interpersonal aspects of good health.

No matter what your status, there are usually things that can be done to enhance health. For example, taking a short walk with a friend can do wonders for your emotional, relational and physical well-being. It's amazing how much can be gained from just fifteen minutes of fresh air, sunshine, and movement. Your individualized regimen can be as rudimentary or complex as your situation will allow. The important thing is to try and do 'something'. For some this may be deciding to get out of bed when it would be all too easy to stay.

On a scale of 1 to 10 (1 being the lowest & 10 the highest), where would you rate your health status?

1 2 3 4 5 6 7 8 9 10

If you would like to increase your rating then please complete the following exercises. If for example, you appraised your health status at (2), what *actions* would you need to take in order to move up to (3)?

_____

_____

_____

_____

_____

_____

* Always consult with your physician before beginning an exercise and/or dietary program.

How will you know when you have reached your goal(s)? What types of *behaviors* will you display that will signal you have moved up to a higher number?

_____

_____

_____

_____

_____

_____

_____

_____

Are you already doing some of these things in your current life (even just a little bit)? If so, what is different about those times? What are you <u>doing</u> differently during those moments? If you still want to change, then I encourage you to do *more* of the healthy things you've identified. In other words, try and *amplify* your success and *expand* your health repertoire. Write about this topic in the space provided below.

_____

_____

_____

_____

_____

_____

Chapter 5

"It is the same light coming through different colors, but in the heart of everything the same truth reigns; I am in every religion as the thread through a string of pearls."

~Vivekananda

The poignant quote by Vivekananda, reminds me of a childhood story, *"The Blind Men and the Elephant."* This fable illustrates six blind men that describe an elephant. Each one touches a different part of the elephant and explains what he feels. Yet all they do is argue because they will not listen to one another. Each foolishly believes that his idea about the elephant is the only correct one. Does this fable remind you of much of the monotheistic dogma and religious intolerance that has been and continues to be so prevalent throughout the world?

Instead of focusing upon common threads (e.g. love & compassion) people bicker about theology and get caught up in legalistic thinking. Why is this so prevalent, when sayings such as the Golden Rule occur in Confucianism, Buddhism, Judaism, and Christianity? I can't tell you how many times I have heard religious leaders make statements such as, "We must grow up, and get rid of our childish ways." Although there are some childlike behaviors that need to be outgrown, as adults, if only we would remember the simple, yet profound lessons taught in childhood parables!

My hope is that this section will provoke reflection on the topic of spirituality. But make no mistake; my writing is not intended to proselytize or convert the reader to any particular theological persuasion. In fact, I am not even suggesting that a theistic point of view is necessary for this chapter to be applicable. With this in mind, I invite you to explore the topic of spirituality by taking some time for introspection. To help facilitate this self-examination, I have provided some questions that you may answer on the next few pages.

What does it mean to be spiritual?

_____

_____

_____

_____

_____

_____

_____

Do you believe that a spiritual connection is an essential ingredient for living and dying?

_____

_____

_____

_____

_____

_____

_____

_____

_____

Is religiosity synonymous with spirituality?

_____

_____

_____

_____

_____

_____

_____

_____

_____

_____

Would you view spirituality in a different light if you had just one year left to live?

_____

_____

_____

_____

_____

_____

_____

_____

_____

_____

Chapter 6

Purposefully live with purpose.

~Eric A. Sleith III

Once upon a time, there was a place called *the land of Nod*. It was appropriately given this name because most of its inhabitants would nod off to sleep every day. People existed, but they did not really *live*. They found the daily routine to be tedious and lackluster. Some lived for work, while others just worked to live. However, both groups had one thing in common; they lacked a sense of purpose in their careers. They simply worked to earn money.

Is this fairy-tale reminiscent of significant others in your social and occupational milieu? If you're honest, do you see a little bit of yourself in the narrative? Although there's a few that truly live with passion and purpose, most are only going through the motions.

What if you we're given a terminal diagnosis and told that you had only twelve-months to live? Would you do something different in your vocation? Would your vocation be transformed into an *avocation*? Many use the terms vocation and avocation interchangeably, but they have very different meanings. A person's vocation is something that they do to maintain employment and earn money, while an avocation is seen as a *calling* and a labor of love. An avocation can earn someone money, but that is not the primary purpose for pursuing a specific path.

There is a well-known motto that says, *"If you do what you love, you'll never have to work a day in your life."* What are you truly passionate about? What is it that puts a sparkle in your eye? What would you attempt if you knew you could not fail? Carefully consider these questions and then write about your thoughts on the subsequent pages.

_____

_____

_____

_____

_____

_____

Chapter 7

Nothing is enough for the man whom enough is too little.

~Epicurus

John D. Rockefeller was once asked, *"How much money does it take to satisfy a man?"* **He responded by saying,** *"Just a little more."* **When he died, his accountant was asked,** *"How much did Mr. Rockefeller leave?"* **The accountant responded by saying,** *"All of it."*

We can't take anything with us!

This chapter is about getting your <u>financial house in order</u>. It is by no means all-inclusive, but will cover some of the most basic topics such as:

1. Living within your means.

2. Creating a budget.

3. Writing a will.

4. Life Insurance

5. Advance Directives.

Our culture has a strange relationship with money. On the one hand, money is idolized and made into a God. On the other, it is seen as the epitome of evil. For instance, many people pursue money at the expense of everything else. They may have a large financial portfolio, but they can usually be described as emotionally, spiritually, and relationally bankrupt. Conversely, you have some that view money as the root of all evil, and spout naive phrases such as, "All we need is love." In my opinion, this creates a false dichotomy that reinforces and perpetuates the two extremes. As with most things in life, a healthy balance is key.

After the Great Depression many people in the United States buried money in their back yards. Not only was this an economic mistake (i.e. going broke due to inflation) but it also instilled a fear-based relationship as it relates to the role of money. Before our current economic recession, most Americans went to the other extreme and lived well beyond their means. Although some people had no other choice than to use credit to purchase food and medicine, many were simply gluttonous and irresponsible.

Let me share a story that illustrates the importance of living with our means. I once heard about a man that earned a gross salary of $36,000 dollars a year. After taxes, health insurance premiums and retirement deductions, his take-home pay equaled about $475 dollars a week. He complained that it was difficult to live on this amount of money in the current day and age. He repeatedly said that if he could only earn $100,000 dollars a year, his money troubles would be over. This man was quite industrious and managed to work his way to the top of the corporate ladder. Within a few years he reached his goal and earned a six-figure salary. However, he soon learned that the taxman visited more often and consumed a much larger piece of his financial pie. In addition, because of his larger salary he decided to reward himself by purchasing a bigger home and a luxury car. His wife began to shop more often too, and she insisted that the children be placed in a private school. Within a short amount of time he realized that he wanted to (he mistakenly believed he "needed to") earn even more money. So he began working longer and longer hours and sacrificed his health and interpersonal relationships. But all of his hard work was not in vain. He eventually earned a quarter of a million dollars a year and had made it to the big leagues! By now, he and Uncle Sam were on a first name basis. When the tax collector came a knocking, he took approximately one half of his earnings. And in order to run with the big boys, he had to play the part. Custom made suits, high priced jewelry and elaborate vacations were no longer the exception but the norm.

In truth, this is a hypothetical story that I made up to prove a point. Even though most of us will never earn $250,000 dollars a year, I believe it's easy to see a little part of ourselves in this character. We should not kid ourselves, if we will not live within our means right where we're at or be a good steward of what we already have, what makes us think we will do any better if we gain more?

Desire has an insatiable appetite!

We must learn how to differentiate between *needs* and *desires*. Just because advertisers tell us that we must have their product, it doesn't mean that we should switch to autopilot and discard rational thought. It is vital that we curb our financial appetite and make decisions that are well considered and not based on impulse or conditioning. One way to accomplish this is through the ritual utilization of a budget. A budget is simply a tool that allows you to keep track of how much money is coming in and going out each month. The primary goal is to live within your means by allocating funds to specific categories. That way you know how much you have to spend in a particular area each month. Most of us have limits on how much money we can bring through the front gate, but we have considerable control over what we throw out the back door. An Internet search will provide numerous examples of budgets that can be used as a template and customized to meet your specific situation. Dave Ramsey offers sound financial advice and free downloads (e.g. Quickie budget from.)

This information can be located at:

http://www.daveramsey.com/

http://www.daveramsey.com/tools/budget-forms/

Other financial and end of life topics that need to be evaluated are: Writing a <u>Will</u> (asset distribution, guardianship for minor children etc.) <u>Life Insurance</u> (whole life vs. term). <u>Advance Directives</u>, which is a general term for any document that directs others about your health care wishes when you can no longer express yourself (e.g. living will, durable power of attorney for health care, etc.) Since I am not an expert on these topics, I recommend that you contact an Estate Attorney, CPA (Certified Public Accountant) and CFP (Certified Financial Planner) for professional consultations. I have included some helpful resources to assist you.

1. The American Bar Association's Tool Kit for Health Care Advance Planning:
   www.abanet.org/aging/toolkit/home.html

2. National Hospice & Palliative Care Organization's List of Advance Directive Forms by State: www.caringinfo.org/stateaddownload

3. AARP Advance Directive Information: www.aarp.org/research

4. Free Legal Forms. www.free-legal-document.com/index.html

5. Board of Standards: http://www.cfp.net/

Chapter 8

Death, stay close to me, so that I may fully embrace life.

~Eric A. Sleith

For many, the thought of death congers up the ultimate notion concerning loss of control. Usually when I encourage someone that is in their youth to plan their own funeral, I am met with resistance. A common response goes something like this, "I am still young, and that's something you do when you get older. Why bother focusing upon such a morbid topic." The typical reaction from someone that's older is, "I have already prepared a will and set enough money aside to pay for the funeral expenses." Both responses reflect the anxiety that most people experience about the topic of death (especially their own) and the tendency to avoid having an in-depth and serious conversation about it.

I strongly believe that when we plan for our own funeral we are taking charge of the things in which we have control over. Although we can try our best to prevent disease and avoid accidents, calamities still occur and there are no guarantees in life. This inevitable fact is what many find so frightening. In my experience, most people want to have a sense of influence and predictability over major life events. This is precisely why I am asking you to plan for your own funeral.

A eulogy is a written and/or verbal statement about someone who has died. Someone that knew the deceased usually writes this final summation. But why should we leave such an important last statement in the hands of someone else? We may not be able to control when or how we die, but we certainly can produce a definitive statement that accurately reflects what we stood for. This final written account represents the culmination of both an arduous and rewarding journey. Please consider the questions then write your own eulogy.

What do you want the world to remember most about you?

_____

_____

_____

_____

_____

What does your life ultimately stand for?

_____

_____

_____

_____

If you had to pick one "symbol" to represent your life, what would it be?

_____

_____

_____

_____

<u>Write your own eulogy</u>

_____

_____

_____

_____

_____

_____

_____

_____

_____

_____

_____

_____

_____

_____

_____

_____

_____

Build Your Own Casket

Although some people purchase a burial plot before they die, far fewer consider constructing their own casket. This can be as simple as building a wood box from scratch or putting together a prefabricated unit. I realize that this idea is not for everyone and may seem quite bizarre. Nevertheless, it is worthy of discussion because it serves two very important functions. First, it offers each of us the freedom to make a choice about what we will be buried in, or if we wish to be buried at all (e.g. cremation). Second, the financial costs can be significantly reduced when building your own casket or purchasing wholesale. Many funeral homes charge between $ 5,000.00 – 10,000.00 just for a casket. Some unscrupulous funeral directors prey upon the grief and guilt of survivors by overselling products and services and charging exorbitant prices. It is important for you to know your options and legal rights on this topic.

Most people are unaware that The Federal Trade Commission (FTC) requires funeral homes to accept any casket purchased from an outside source. (See the FTC website http://www.ftc.gov/) What this means for the consumer is that a funeral provider may not refuse or charge a fee, if you decide to purchase a casket from somewhere else. There are several places that sell high quality, yet inexpensive products that can be delivered overnight. (See websites below)

http://www.costco.com/ (Go to Funeral then click on Caskets or Urns.)

http://casketxpress.com/

http://www.ehow.com/how_2100021_build-casket.html
(This website teaches you how to build your own casket).

Currently, caskets can be purchased from and shipped to addresses in the following states: Arizona, California, Colorado, Connecticut, District of Columbia, Florida, Illinois, Indiana, Iowa, Kansas, Kentucky, Massachusetts, Michigan, Missouri, Montana, Nebraska, Nevada, New Hampshire, New Jersey, New Mexico, New York, North Carolina, North Dakota, Ohio, Oregon, Pennsylvania, South Dakota, Tennessee, Texas, Utah, Washington, West Virginia, Wisconsin and Wyoming.

Chapter 9

We're all just passing through, so enjoy each stop along the way.

~Eric A. Sleith III

There was a man who was traveling far away from home. He stopped into a restaurant and the waitress asked, "Do you live around here or are you just passing through?" This man was a deep thinker and so he considered her question on multiple levels. At first, he thought about responding with a simple and straightforward answer. But he sensed that this woman was not your typical waitress, so he replied by saying, *"Aren't we all just passing through."* This was a rhetorical question, and from the look on her face, he knew that she understood the underlying meaning and existential implications.

I am very fond of the word *"sojourner."* This beautiful phrase encapsulates the essence of this chapter and reminds me that we are all passing through, if only for a moment. To put things in perspective, I'd like to present some basic facts about the age of our earth and the typical lifespan of human beings. Most geologists agree that the age of the earth is approximately four and one half billion years. In contrast, the average human life lasts only between seventy-five to eighty years. If you really think about it, in the grand scheme of things, we are here and gone within the blink of an eye. But that does not mean that we should despair. It simply reminds us of our ephemeral existence and invites us to live with a full and open heart before passing on.

From nowhere we came; into nowhere we go. What is life? It is the flash of a firefly in the night. It is the breath of a buffalo in the winter time. It is as the little shadow that runs across the grass and loses itself in the sunset.

~Crowfoot, Blackfoot tribe

If you only had a short time to live, what would be the ten places you'd most want to visit or things you'd like to do before dying? Please take some time to reflect and then create your own personalized *"Must see and do"* list.

1. _____

2. _____

3. _____

4. _____

5. _____

6. _____

7. _____

8. _____

9. _____

10. _____

Afterword

We are all in the process of dying, but how many of us can say we are really living.

~Eric A. Sleith III

At the beginning of this book I asked you to imagine having a near death experience. I now request that you allow your mind to dream, one last time. Imagine that you are in a doctor's office; no, not the examination room, but the doctor's personal office. You realize that if she asked you to meet in *'there'* to discuss the test results, then it must be bad. Your physician tries her best to appear hopeful, but you can see the truth in her eyes. Her tone of voice and non-verbal behavior communicates one thing; you are going to die. Finally, after swimming through the murky waters of statistics and medical nomenclature, you arrive at the "bottom line." As you leave the doctors office, all you can remember is one sentence that keeps repeating over and over in your mind, "You have about twelve months to live." You fanaticize about a giant red marker crossing out another day, then month by month being torn from the pages of your final calendar. It's your last spring, Fourth of July fireworks, dragonflies and crickets, and humid summer nights. Finally as the seasons change, you visualize the falling autumn leaves and the impending cold and dark winter. But even though death looms like a cloud over a mountaintop, there is a clarity and sharpness to "life" that has never before been experienced! It's as if you are seeing things for the first time. Really seeing them, not just going through the motions, but being completely present and in the moment. Sure you've heard about living in the moment before, but you never understood what it really meant, until now. Colors are more vibrant and your sense of smell is heightened. This is not just life, in the physical sense of the word, but this represents being immersed in "living." Why did it have to take dying to understand this important life lesson? So many years wasted, so much time lost.

For some, this exercise is reminiscent of a vivid dream gone awry, which dissipates like the morning fog that is burned away by the rising sun. For others, this nightmare is all too real. Regardless of which group you belong, there is one common denominator that unites us all. Each of us must face the awesome responsibility of choosing what to do with the time we have been given. There are no promises that we will see all the seasons of our lives, so we must make the most of each precious moment!

Strive to be alive.....not just to stay alive.

~Eric A. Sleith III

He who has a 'why' to live for can bear almost any 'how'.

~Nietzsche

Checklist

Attorney ( )   Will ( )   CPA ( )

CFP ( )   Physician ( )   Dietitian ( )

Counselor ( )   Budget ( )   List of Goals ( )

Advance Directives ( )   Mission Statement ( )

Life Insurance ( )   Top-Ten List ( )

Exercise Regimen ( )   Occupational Plan ( )

Spiritual Advisor ( )   Funeral Preparations ( )

* Use this list to help you keep track of what's been completed and what still needs to be done on your journey.

Thank You!

I want to thank you for spending your hard earned money on this publication. I realize there are millions of books to choose from and I am honored that you selected this title. If this workbook helped you in some way, please consider sharing your experience with others by writing a review on http://www.amazon.com, etc.

Sincerely,

Eric

www.ingramcontent.com/pod-product-compliance
Lightning Source LLC
Chambersburg PA
CBHW081404280526
45788CB00009B/2977